How do children with disabilities experience poverty, disability and service delivery?

A REPORT ON PARTICIPATORY WORKSHOPS

GLYNIS CLACHERTY, KGETHI MATSHAI AND WASHEILA SAIT

2004

idasa

10 years of democracy

Produced by the Children's Budget Unit of Idasa's Budget Information Service

Clacherty & Associates

**Education and Social Development (Pty) Ltd
PO Box 613, Auckland Park, 2006, South Africa**

The research was undertaken by Kgethi Matshai, Jessie Kgomongoe and Glynis Clacherty. Washeila Sait helped facilitate the Western Cape workshop and reviewed the report.

Published by Idasa, 6 Spin St, Cape Town 8001

© Idasa

ISBN 1-919798-62-5   ISBN-13: 978-1-919798-62-2

First published in 2004

Editing by Bronwen Müller

Design and layout by Bronwen Müller

Cover by Mandy Darling, Magenta Media

The illustrations in this report and on the cover are taken from activities children did in the participatory research groups.

Printed by Lightning Source

Contents

Background

Idasa's Children's Budget Unit (CBU) in partnership with the South African Federal Council on Disability (SAFCD) has produced a study that provides information on government programmes, government budget allocations and spending for children with disabilities.

It was important that this study involve children for, as Ivan-Smith and Johnson (1998 p.299) point out:

> If we are unaware of the problems and issues that concern children and young people we cannot hope to devise strategies or solutions that will address their concerns.

Participatory workshops were held around South Africa with children who have disabilities. This report is based on the information gathered in these workshops.

It is important to note that the children and disability budget study is a broad one and that the research with disabled children focused only on the children's experience of poverty, disability and existing service provision.

Also, it is equally important to understand the context in which the term "disability" is used, since it will provide a better understanding of the barriers that disabled children experience in terms of equal opportunity and development.

Disability is the loss or limitations of opportunities to take part in the normal life of the community on an equal level with others due to physical and social barriers (Barnes: 1999).

Research approach

The research approach was a qualitative one that consisted of a series of participatory workshops in which children were encouraged to talk about their lives. These discussions were recorded and transcribed.

In the participatory workshops we sought to allow children to participate in a meaningful way. Boyden and Ennew (1997) point out that if children's participation is to be more than token the following issues need to be taken into account:

- Ethical issues in research with relatively powerless groups;

- The capacities of children at different ages and stages of development.

The research was devised in such a way as to take particular ethical issues into account. In addition, the activities used in the research workshops were suited to the ages and stages of development of the children.

Ethical issues

The ethical guidelines for research work with children used by participatory researchers internationally was applied in this research (see Appendix 1). In addition, three other key ethical principles informed the participatory workshops with children:

- Minimising harm;

- Benefit to the participants;

- Feedback and follow up.

  It is not ethical to expose a child already vulnerable to any additional risk through an investigation that carries no benefit for the child. Interviews about painful subjects should be performed with the principle of "least harm" (Boyden and Ennew, 1997, p.43).

i) Minimising harm

We tried to make sure that all children we worked with as part of this study were part of an ongoing support programme. This is important because, despite the fact that researchers clarify to the best of their ability that they cannot provide direct personal help, it is often the case that some children harbour unrealistic expectations of the research interaction (cf. Johnson, 1996). It is important, therefore, to have a mechanism with which to provide support for children after the research. Any issues raised in the research groups that we, as researchers, felt needed further work were referred to the staff from the support organisation.

Researchers who ran the focus group discussions were aware that the discussions we held could touch on sensitive and difficult issues for many children. The principle of "minimising harm" was applied throughout. Practically this meant that researchers made it possible for children to withdraw at any stage, were sensitive about issues which may have caused shame or embarrassment, did not challenge the child about answers given, and did not ask questions which could be upsetting. They also created an environment in which children could tell just as much of their story as they felt safe to tell. They did not probe about the details of a painful event, nor ask about a child's feelings. When the child told a painful story what the child offered was accepted, even if not all the details were present.

Also, complete confidentiality of data was another way in which we sought to minimise harm. Children's names were recorded for follow-up purposes only. This is why descriptors instead of names are used to identify quotes in the report. The names of children in the short case studies have been changed.

ii) Benefit to participating children

In terms of benefit to the child, there is much international and local experience (Dawes, 2000) that suggests that children benefit from participatory processes. Evidence suggests that taking part in a process such as this one contributes to building children's self-esteem and encourages self-reflection, and that talking about a problem allows children to organise their perceptions about how to solve it.

Informal discussion with children who took part in this research suggests that they felt valued because they were being asked their opinions. The transcripts of discussion in the focus groups show the reflection and problem-solving process described above.

iii) Feedback and follow up

Records were kept that will enable later contact with the children involved in the research. Any later contact will maintain confidentiality and not give out real names of persons or organisations without informed consent. The aim of keeping the record is primarily to ensure that children can be contacted where further intervention is required, but also to facilitate further research if appropriate.

We will ensure that adequate feedback is given to the children involved in the research regarding the outcome of the research. This will be done through a simple newsletter that describes to the children who participated what has happened to the report and tells them a little about the process of advocacy that is involved in the Idasa Children's Budget project.

Participants in the research

In order to represent the needs of different children a range of disabilities was represented within the following categories in the workshops:

- Deafness;
- Blindness;
- Mental and neurological disabilities;
- Physical disabilities;
- Chronic conditions.

Girls and boys were mixed in all the workshops.

Five activity-based workshops were held in five provinces: KwaZulu-Natal, Eastern Cape, Limpopo, Western Cape and North West. At least eight children attended each workshop. Three focus group discussions were also held with caregivers in three areas.

To ensure that we heard the voices of children in different circumstances they were accessed through several organisations. Apart from the KwaZulu-Natal group, which was run in a Department of Education boarding school, the groups were set up through local community-based organisations such as the Disabled Children's Action Group (Dicag).

The table below describes the different circumstances of these groups in more detail. More information is given about the children themselves in the tables in Appendix 2.

Caregiver groups were conducted in Limpopo, North West and the Eastern Cape. The caregivers were the parents, carers and teachers of the children who attended the research workshops.

KwaZulu-Natal	**Children who were attending St Martin's School for deaf and physically disabled children in Port Shepstone.** This group all attended school. All but one of the eight children was boarding at the school as they lived far away from the school. The children came from a mix of rural and urban areas all over KwaZulu-Natal.
Western Cape	**An informal group organised by Dicag, Western Cape.** The children in this group came from the Cape Town area, except for one boy who came from a commercial farm in the Ceres area. All the children, apart from the boy in the Ceres area and one other, were attending local schools.
Eastern Cape	**An informal group organised through Disa (Disabled Sports Association).** The children in this group came from East London and areas around it. Three of the children came from a shack area in Duncan Village just outside of town, one boy from Amalinda a suburb in town. Two children came from Mdantsane, one girl came from Mooiplaas which is a rural area about 35km from town, and one boy came from Dimbaza, near King William's Town. Four of the children in this group were in school and four were not.
Limpopo	**A group organised through a community centre for children with disabilities run by local volunteers.** The children we worked with came from Botlokwa, a village about 55km from Polokwane. It is a peri-urban area with a hospital and many schools. The school is run by volunteers and relies heavily on donations.
North West	**An informal group organised by Dicag, North West.** Two of the children in this group came from Moretele and Makapanstad, which are villages in and around Hammanskraal, and the rest came from a community centre in Themba, an urban township near Hammanskraal in the former Bophuthatswana homeland.

Research activities

A workshop outline that included activities suited to the age and stage of development of the children involved was devised. It is important to note that activities were adapted according to the children's particular needs and abilities. Groups were conducted in the language/s of the group members, by multilingual researchers.

The table on the next page gives an outline of the workshop activities followed in all the groups. The activities were introduced with "getting to know you" games and were interspersed with breaks for refreshments, etc.

Data analysis

All the research workshops were run in the home language of the participants. The discussion in all these workshops was taped in order to capture the authentic voices of the children. The researcher who ran the workshop then transcribed the tapes, translating

How do children with disabilities experience poverty, disability and service delivery?

Activity	Procedure	Aims
Activity 1: My day	Participants were asked to draw what they did yesterday – beginning with yesterday gives more accurate information than asking in general terms about a typical day. Children will then each describe what they have drawn. Working from the example of yesterday the researcher then asked questions about other days i.e. weekends and holidays to get a sense of what happens on other days. Researchers probed around access to service provision, for example, they found out which children go to school and which do not and why. They also looked at the access children have to health care. **Alternative** Children were given playdough or clay and asked to make three shapes that show their day – the start of their day, the middle and the end. Using these shapes as a starting point the researcher then interacted with the children around what they do during a typical day.	• To find out what activities children do. • To find out how children with disabilities spend their time. • To find out which services they have access to.
Activity 2: Problems in my day	Children were asked to take small round pieces of paper and draw on to them the problems they face in their day. They then stuck these on to the drawing at the appropriate place. If the children used playdough, problems were discussed in relation to the playdough day rather than the drawing. Researchers then discussed the different problems and found out from the group how common the particular problem was.	• To find out what problems children experience on a daily basis.
Activity 3: My place	Using playdough, children made small figures of themselves and of the other people they interact with every day. These were placed on the floor or on a table and then, using matchboxes for houses and cut-out paper buildings such as school, clinic, social worker's office, church etc, the researchers and children built a three-dimensional "map" of the community the children live in. The "map" was then discussed looking particularly at the access children have to local services and how they interact with children and adults in the community. Researchers probed around access to services through looking at places in the community such as the school and clinic. **Alternative** Children drew a "map" of their area.	• To find out how children with disabilities are integrated or not in their local communities and what services they use.
Activity 4: My strengths and needs	A packet with marshmallows and (clean) stones in it was passed around the circle. The children were told that there were two things in the packet: 1. Marshmallows that stand for the good things in their life (the things that help them.) They can be things inside themselves like determination and they can also be things outside like a granny who cares. 2. Stones that stand for things they do not have that they need – or their problems. As the packet was passed around the children talked about the good things and difficult things in their lives. Researchers probed around the coping strategies they draw on, on an individual level, and what help they get from families, people in the community, the church, the school and also tried to understand any way they draw on institutions like local government. Researchers also probed around how children think these services could be provided for them in a way that they would be able to access.	• To allow the children to describe what they have to draw on to help them solve their problems – what are their existing coping strategies? • What services they think government could provide for them. • How they think these services should be provided for them.

into English as part of the transcription process. The aim in the translation was to keep the sentence structure and form of expression as close to the original as possible. When a phrase was not easily translated, usually because it was idiomatic, it was transcribed in the original.

These transcripts formed the data and were subjected to thematic analysis. Several themes were generated inductively from the raw material, i.e. they were allowed to emerge through reading and re-reading the transcripts. The themes that emerged reflect the pattern of experience of all the different groups we worked with. Where there were noticeable differences between groups, these have been highlighted in the report.

Extensive use is made of quotes from the transcripts. This is to allow the children's unique experiences to be heard.

Findings

The findings are presented within eight themes, which emerged from discussions with the children and with caregivers. Caregivers included parents, teachers and others at school or home.

- Poverty;
- Schooling;
- Abuse;
- Social security;
- Health care and services;
- Participation, socialisation and recreation;
- Discrimination and acceptance;
- Family support.

These themes illustrate not only the barriers that disabled children face on a daily basis, but also the resilience they demonstrate in coping within a disabling environment and their ability to make a contribution to society if given equal opportunities and access to socio-economic rights.

The case study on the next page, written from the researcher's notes, highlights many of these themes. It illustrates the many obstacles that children with disabilities face as well as their resilience and the contribution they could make in our society if only services were available.

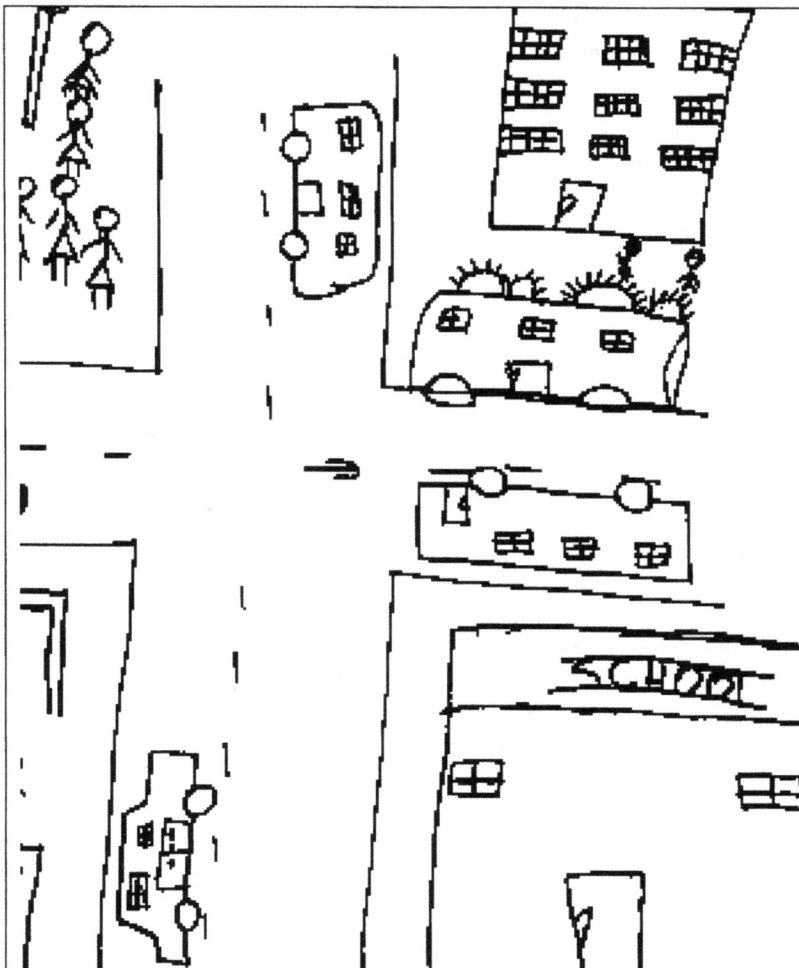

Johanna's story (From researcher's notes)

Johanna is a 14-year-old girl, who lives at Makapanstad near Hammanskraal in North West province. She lives with her father, mother and two younger siblings. Both her parents are unemployed, and her two younger siblings are in school.

According to her mother, Johanna started having problems when she was young. She cannot name the disability she has but there seems to be physical and intellectual disability of some sort. She did not cope in a mainstream school so then attended the local community centre for children with disabilities that is run by Dicag. She no longer attends as she fell from a bus one day when she came back from school and she stayed in hospital for many weeks. Since this accident she is afraid to go on a bus again and because of this she does not go to school anymore.

Johanna is a beautiful girl with a beautiful body. She is light in complexion and has a lovely smile. When you look closely at her you see the smile is combined with a frown. It is always there. When she starts moving you realise that it is not easy for her to move her hand and foot on her right side. She struggles with speech although you can hear what she is saying.

Johanna is lively and talkative. In the group she thought deeply about the questions we asked and asked questions that clarified things further for herself. Once she understood she would beam and start responding to the question animatedly and enthusiastically.

At times she panicked when she did not understand what was being said. When this happened she quickly called her mother who came, told her to calm down and then to listen. Johanna did this with ease. There is an understanding between her and her mother. They know each other well. You can see from the mother's eyes that she cares deeply for her daughter. They spend a lot of time together and there is this deeper understanding that's admirable. Her mother can tell from looking at Johanna whether she understands what is happening around her or not. She can even tell when Johanna knows the answer to the question being asked. She reassures her and supports her and this gives Johanna confidence and strength. If Johanna says "I can't do this", her mother is able to say to her, "You can do it. Just listen". You can actually see Johanna relax. Then she will look at her mother, smile, listen to what is being asked, ask more questions and then start thinking about her response.

Johanna was in the group for a while with Jessie (the other researcher) and I joined the group with children from another school who had arrived late. Johanna was happy to see them and immediately made them feel at ease. She talked to them and told them what she had been doing with Jessie. When we started working with the other children she was attentive and helped us to explain to them. She could see when others could not understand and helped them out. She was good at this. She thinks hard about what she does.

Johanna comes from a very poor home and her condition is in many ways made worse by her circumstances. This is coupled with the fact that the parents are not readily able to tell you exactly what the doctors say the problem is. Her parents have tried several times to apply for a Care Dependency Grant for Johanna as they feel the money would help them find an appropriate school. Her mother says clerks, social workers and doctors are divided on whether Johanna qualifies for the grant. The local social worker has advised her mother that nothing can be done for Johanna now and that she should simply wait until she is 18 then apply again and maybe then will she get the grant. At present they are waiting for Johanna to reach 18 and they are hoping that she will qualify for the grant.

In the meantime Johanna sits at home, desperately wanting to go to school.

Theme A: Poverty

One significant theme that emerged from discussions was the poverty that many of the children live in. The depth of this poverty became obvious when children talked about the things they need but do not have. In the Eastern Cape, Limpopo and North West some children in each group talked about being hungry.

> At school what is good is the food. Sometimes there is nothing at home. (North West)

Obviously hunger has a physiological effect on growing children but there are other effects too. The emotional impact of hunger is obvious from quotes such as this:

> – Sometimes I am angry.
>
> – What makes you angry?
>
> – Being hungry. (Limpopo)

Caregivers also talked about hunger.

> The families who send their children to the centre they struggle. You will find they don't get grant and no one is working in the house. You will see the people are suffering from hunger. You can even see the child enjoys to be at school more than home because at least they do get something to eat. How can you ask them for school fees? Other people are living in the worst situation. Sometimes the children tell you how many days they sleep without getting food. You feel sad after hearing those stories. (Caregiver, North West)

> But you find when the school is near the closing date there are those who cry, who do not want to go home because they only get meals here at school. We serve two meals here at school. Some have only these meals because of circumstances at home, difficulties, so they do not want to go home. (Teacher, Eastern Cape)

> When J (child) is hungry she cannot speak or do anything. (Mother, North West)

Apart from hunger, poverty affects the lives of the children in other ways too. Small and cramped homes are an issue for children with disabilities, particularly wheelchair users.

> If I want to make myself something to eat, I can do that – make my own food and stuff, but if I try the kitchen is too tight. There is no space for the wheelchair. And if I want to go outside, we have a ramp but I sometimes get stuck. I cannot move around the house easily. (Western Cape)

> I stay in one room in the house because it is not accessible. I am struggling to get to my room or anywhere else in the house. The house is very small. (Western Cape)

Poverty also affects schooling.

> I could not go to school for a month because the grant did not come and I did not have money for taxis. (KwaZulu-Natal)

Theme B: Schooling

A significant issue for many of the children who participated in this study was that they did not have access to adequate schooling. Four of the children in this study were not attending school at all. This interaction between a girl in North West and a researcher shows how the child experiences being out of school.

> – When I wake up I brush my teeth. I prepare water and then I make tea. I wash the dishes. I wash the clothes. I wash the school uniform of my little brother when he comes from school.
>
> – Yo! You wash the dishes! You are a hard worker. What else do you do?
>
> – I sit.
>
> – You sit?
>
> – Yes. I sit with my mom.
>
> – You don't go to school?
>
> – No.
>
> – Is there a school near where you are staying?
>
> – We do have school. It is only for children who are normal, who have everything in their body – those who are full in their bodies.
>
> – So who says you are not full in your body?
>
> – They say so when they tease me. I was attending school for normal children but they tease me and I am not attending anymore.
>
> – Do you want to go to school?
>
> – I want to go to school. Hey, hey, I do get bored. I get very angry when I see other children going to school. I don't feel good when I don't go to school.
>
> – It makes you sad when you don't go to school?
>
> – I feel sad and angry when I don't go to school. I am growing but I don't have the knowledge. People my age are all going to school. I just sit.

A girl from the Western Cape describes her day without school.

> – In the morning I wake up, I go to the bathroom and wash me, dress me and I watch TV. I go to the park with my dogs sometimes and then I go home.
>
> – Do you go to school?
>
> – No, I am out of school.
>
> – Why are you not going to school?
>
> – I can't learn further. I was in a school where they learn you to clean the house and make food and so on. But they said I could not go further.
>
> – Would you like to go to school?

> – Yes. I would like just to do school work, do Maths and English and all the work. I just sit at home and watch TV, it would be better at school. (18-year-old, Western Cape)

The issue of schooling concerns more than disabled children attending school, however. Thirteen of the children in the groups that were run were going to school, but they were not schools that could meet their educational needs adequately. They were in local mainstream schools where they were being "kept busy" rather than educated, or in informal community centres run by local volunteers who were usually the mothers of children with disabilities.

> They are doing activities with them like cleaning the school and singing but they are not learning. (Mother, Limpopo)

> But at the moment there is no school for him, his problem is not sorted out. For now he is going to the school he used to go to (the local mainstream school) that is nearby so they can keep him busy. They just allow him to go there but there isn't much that is being done. (Mother, Eastern Cape)

Disabled children in urban areas have more opportunity to access appropriate education than those in rural areas. This was clearly demonstrated among the Western Cape respondents (Cape Town), which had the highest proportion of children in schools that were able to cater for their needs appropriately. Within this same group, one of the respondents lives within a rural area outside of Cape Town and does not attend school because there is no school within his area that could adequately provide for his specific needs as he has a progressive muscular disorder.

One group was run with children who were in a boarding school in Port Shepstone. This school offers a broad range of specialised education, including appropriate services for deaf children. The children in this group described how important school was to them.

> I love it here at school. I have friends who understand me and we can learn to talk to each other in Sign. We learn a lot. (KwaZulu-Natal)

It was clear to researchers that the children in this group (as well as the children from Cape Town who were attending school) were more confident and articulate and able to express their needs and experiences more easily than the children in informal learning situations or not in school at all.

One child, who was not in school at all, expressed why education was especially important for her as a child with a disability. When asked to talk about something that is a problem in her life she said:

> I worry about death. Death is a problem. My mother she is very important. She wash me, brush my hair, she do everything that she can for me. If she goes away I will look for her and follow her. If I can't find her I will cry. I worry about death. But I am not going to school. Other children my age are getting knowledge but I am not going to school. (North West)

Her mother's comments cast light on why this girl is afraid of death.

> I am worried about her age. She also worries about her age and she is worried that one day I am going to die. She is able to see that she is growing up and has no education. She knows I am going to die and her father will die. She says to me, "You will be gone and I won't be able to write or do something for myself. Who is going to help me?" She is disabled but her brain can function and she asks hard questions that always hurt me. She says, "Imagine if I will be staying alone because my younger brother will be married". (North West)

This idea was reiterated by a young woman in the Cape Town group. She had recently left school because she had reached the highest grade that the school in her area offered. She wanted schooling that would provide her with vocational skills.

> I want to learn so I can get a job one day. But they say the school cannot take me any more. What am I going to do to earn money? I will need a job one day. (Western Cape)

Caregivers also talked about this issue.

> One other sad thing is that at age 18 we are expected to discharge children. They go and sit in the township. There is no other programme that caters for them beyond. All of a sudden he does not have anything to do. He used to be a good sportsman here at school, then as he goes back to the township the skills he has acquired die. (Caregiver, Eastern Cape)

One girl attended a mainstream school. This is how she described her experience of school.

> – I go to the mainstream school. I have been in mainstream all my life, from pre-school. I do not have any problems at school. The children all accept me, and the teachers.
>
> – Can you move around your school easily? Is it a double-storey school?
>
> – It is, but they have moved all my classes to the ground floor and I have ramps for other stairs. I have no problems getting around. (Western Cape)

Caregivers expressed the difficulties in finding appropriate schooling for their children's specific learning needs.

> He was once in a normal school but they said they cannot cope with him. They will need teachers who are special to help him. But at the moment there is no school for him near here. (Eastern Cape)

A pattern that emerges when caregivers talk about schooling is one where parents struggle to find an appropriate school and keep moving their children from one school to another. Most do not find the specialised education their children need.

> A was in a normal school but her problem is the eyes. She is slow in writing and never finishes what she is doing. She says teachers are impatient with her. But eventually we realised the teachers have a problem with her, they also tell us. So we sent her to P, a school for the blind. But it was difficult for her there; she could not cope in the hostel. She saw bad things that were not supposed to be done by other children. So we took her out of hostel and she went to stay with her aunt. There was transport that was fetching her from home. The aunt was not satisfied with the school. She could not see anything happening. Weeks went by without seeing any work the children were doing. We gave up and brought her back. We took her to the doctors. Doctors said that as well as her partial blindness there is also a problem in her head. We had to find a school for blindness and that problem too. (Mother, Eastern Cape)

Another theme that emerged from the caregivers' focus group discussion was that finding a school suited to the needs of their child was closely related to a specific diagnosis of the child's disability. Many caregivers had only a vague idea of what the child's disability was.

In the case of physical impairments, such as spina bifida, and sensory impairments such as blindness and deafness, as well as other more obvious physical impairments, children and parents were able to name the disability, which made sourcing the correct education and intervention easier. In the cases of children with mental and neurological disabilities such as mental illness, intellectual or learning disabilities, or chronic conditions such as epilepsy, very few caregivers had ever been given an accurate diagnosis. Most referred to their children as "slow" or having a "problem in the head".

> They say, "We don't take children who are disabled like yours. We take those who are physically disabled. We are not working with mentally disturbed. Maybe you should look for another place around your area." (Mother, Limpopo)

Teachers described how parents often misunderstood disability.

> When they are told the child doesn't cope they do not accept even when the child is here in this school. We have a problem of parents who are expecting their children to get out of this school. It's as if children are brought here for fixing and then they are ready to go back to the mainstream. They think it is temporary. They are expecting we will teach the children to have brains and take them back to proper schools, that there is something wrong that we can put in the brain to fix it. (Eastern Cape)

Another issue children raised was that the teachers they had come across in both mainstream and "special needs schools" were not always able to cope with their particular disability. They described teachers getting impatient with them and expecting too much from them.

> The teachers do not give you enough time to think. They pass on while you are thinking. They ask the other child while you are still thinking. They can beat you. The teachers get impatient with us. (Child in special school, Eastern Cape)

> They beat you at the school where I was because you do not understand. (Limpopo)

Not all teachers are impatient, however.

> There are those teachers who are able to explain to you when you have not understood it. Who take their time. Those who will say something in English and explain it in Xhosa. (Eastern Cape)

Caregivers also raised the issue of a shortage of trained teachers.

> My problem is at the centre we don't have teachers who are trained for these children. (Caregiver, North West)

A focus group discussion was run with some teachers from one of the special schools in the Eastern Cape. These teachers described their own sense of inadequacy and lack of skills with children with disabilities. They also talked about the need for appropriate curricula.

> I am one of the teachers from a mainstream school. I was teaching one of the boys there (in the mainstream school) who is now here. I couldn't understand that boy. I was beating him to hell. He would defy me. I used to say he was stubborn, disruptive, naughty. That is until I got training in remedial education. When we did work on mental retardation I began to understand him. By this time he was already gone in my school. So teachers cannot stand these children. (Teacher, Eastern Cape)

> As teachers we are not so qualified. We do know something but we need help from outside. I wish that we had help teaching them vocational skills. The Department of Labour needs to help us as teachers. These children

> could do these things like building. But the problem is that our curriculum for them is not appropriate. It says we must teach academics and book work. They cannot do this. (Teacher, Eastern Cape)

They also talked about the issue of age and schooling.

> The other big issue is that according to a circular we are not allowed to take children at the school who are 13 and above. They say these children are already old. What if that child is diagnosed as having a problem at the age of 13 at school? That means the child is sent home with the prospect of doing nothing else. An example, here at school amongst the children on the waiting list, there was a child who had been waiting for five years. When a space came up he was 14 and we were unable to take him. (Teacher, Eastern Cape)

Related to the issue of school is transport to school. In describing their day the children who were attending school all described their transport to school as important and one of the things that helped them and made their lives easier.

> The taxi went to different places to fetch other children to come to school. We are all using it to come to school and to go home. (Limpopo)

> I go to school in the bus. It picks us all up and we go to school together. (Western Cape)

The difficulties these children would face if they had to rely on public transport are highlighted by a young wheelchair user who described the difficulties she faced when wanting to use a taxi.

> The problem is the clinic is very far and when I am going there or going home, the driver don't allow me to go in there with the chair. They say I must pay an extra seat. I have to close the chair and pay an extra seat. (KwaZulu-Natal)

Theme C: Abuse

Another theme that emerged in the groups run with children and caregivers was that children with disabilities often experience abuse. This abuse can take many forms. During discussions in the workshops it became clear that one boy was working more than he should be at home. He identified work as a problem for him.

> When I come home from school I normally have lots of work to do. I clean the house, I wash the fridge, dishes...
> Lots of problems did happen at home. Many things happen at home like to make you work too much or too hard without a break. They have to let you get a break...
> I have to get a break. I must not work too much. (Limpopo)

Given the fact that this research with children was done in a single workshop run by strangers it is understandable that the children did not talk about other forms of abuse.

It is also important to note that children with disabilities are unlikely to talk about abuse because they are less likely to be believed than able-bodied children. This response promotes the "passivity" often described by those who have worked to help children with disabilities to report abuse.

Caregivers and teachers did, however, recount stories about some of the children that relate to sexual abuse and neglect.

> We need social workers in this school. Our children have problems that they tell us. Like B in the group one morning she said, "Miss, there is a brother who called me when I get off the bus." I asked, "What did you do?" "I didn't go." "Did you tell your mother?" "I didn't". There was another child who was abused by someone in the family. You'll just hear her comment in class, "Shu andidinwe! Khange andilalise uboetbanibani." (Shu I am so tired! So and so didn't give me a chance to sleep.) You go to the family and they dismiss what the child is saying as rubbish. They don't want to admit. (Teacher, Eastern Cape)
>
> The other child in the group, T. He gets a grant and the money is used to take care of the children in the mainstream schools. They don't buy them what they need or pay their school fees. When you ask about the grant they say they used the money for the other children's fees and transport. Here is T, he does not even have a shirt to come to school with but he is the one who is getting the grant. When I ask him about it he tells you, "Haai Miss, they are my brothers and sisters, they have to be taken care of. I have to think for them too and take care of them too". (Teacher, Eastern Cape)

(Note: These cases were being dealt with on an ongoing basis by the local organisations who work with the children.)

One of the teachers in the Eastern Cape described how she perceives the children's lives.

> There is no way you can start in a class on a normal day without singing, playing. The children have got so much anger in the morning, baggage. They are angry because the other siblings were given pocket money and they were not given. They are angry because they have been called names, "cripple/stupids" (sdalwa) in the morning. They are angry because they were not taken to the bus stop. It is not safe for them in the shacks, they are dragged into the shacks and abused. Their parents know this but they do not walk to the stop with them. The other children's school clothes were washed but theirs were not. (Teacher, Eastern Cape)

Children also raised the issue of being misunderstood at home and inappropriately handled.

> My mother yells at me and says I like the street too much. (North West)
>
> My aunt says I am stubborn, that's why she beats me. (Limpopo)

This lack of understanding extended to the community.

> They beat us in the taxi. They say we are stubborn, that is why they beat us. (Limpopo)

A big issue around abuse is being labelled stubborn and difficult. Most often it seems that this arises from a lack of ability to communicate. This is a particular issue for deaf children. Deaf children were clear about the need for hearing adults and children to learn some sign language so they could communicate with them as they felt this would reduce the discrimination against them.

> – Tell the government to teach the other schools the sign language.

> – Yes!
>
> – Then people would understand and not call us stubborn.
>
> – So they can communicate with us. (KwaZulu-Natal)

In addition to these issues children raised issues in the groups that related to all children and not only to disability. In the Western Cape group children were concerned about crime.

> One problem is crime in our areas. Too many people get shot. (Western Cape, this boy's father was shot and killed the previous year)

Theme D: Social security

Some children in the groups were accessing the Care Dependency Grant. This money was used to pay school fees and in some cases supplement the family income too. A number of children were not receiving grants of any kind. A few told of the struggles they had to access the grant.

> My mother has gone to the social workers and they say she must come back. We do not get anything. (North West)
>
> I am waiting for the grant. I have been waiting a long time. My mother does not say why. (KwaZulu-Natal)
>
> Sometimes it stops and they tell my mother to fill in new forms. When I do not get it we sometimes have no taxi money for school. (KwaZulu-Natal)

Caregivers also talked about their struggle to access the Care Dependency Grant. Very often this is related to problems concerning the correct diagnosis of disability.

> The problem is that we both don't work, her father and me. She is 14 years old. I ask help from the government so that she can get something so that I can send her to school. The doctor agrees that this child can get a grant and some of the social workers. But some don't agree that she can get a grant. They say she must wait until she is 18. I still try to get help from the social worker...They keep sending me to different places but I still don't get help. (Mother, North West)

Another issue was the discrimination many children with disabilities experience because of the lack of information parents have about how to access schemes such as the poverty reduction programme.

> I am struggling to get the grant. I don't get help at all. We are suffering from hunger. When J (child) is hungry she cannot speak or do anything. She becomes very sick. Some people do get food parcels but when I go to get food parcels (from the social workers) I am not allowed to. I don't under-stand what you have to do to qualify. (Mother, North West)

This last quote makes clear the fact that it is the children outside of the social security system who experience the greatest difficulties.

Theme E: Health care and services

Another theme that emerged from the children's discussions was the issue of appropriate health care services. They related accounts of how difficult it was to access clinics and hospitals.

> We wait in the queue for a long time and then the medicine for me is not there. They push each other in the queue and the people like to go first. (KwaZulu-Natal)

> The problem is the clinic is very far and when I am going there or going home, the driver don't allow me to go in there with the chair. (KwaZulu-Natal)

They also talked about attitudinal barriers that they face at local clinics and hospitals.

> Sometimes the sisters shout at you. We feel sad. I am sick when they are shouting, shouting. (KwaZulu-Natal)

In addition to problems with access to basic health services, a concern raised by disabled children and caregivers related to rehabilitation. Caregivers talked about this.

> We need someone to show us how to help these children with physio. How to improve their bodies. We do not know. (Caregiver, North West)

> When she was in hospital her arm was better. They did exercises but I do not know what to do now. (Parent, Limpopo)

> I do not know how to look after him properly. I need education and to find out what I can do to help. (Parent, Western Cape)

The children in the rural groups and in the informal centres were the worst off in terms of specialised medical care. Most of the children in the Western Cape and KwaZulu-Natal groups had access to rehabilitation services, partly because of their proximity to a metropolitan centre.

Low levels of psychosocial support for children with disabilities also emerged as an issue. A few children expressed the need for emotional support, for example, one child who had been disabled through a bus accident described her fear of the bus.

> I hate to climb in that bus. I am shaking all over. I remember that day when I had the accident. This is why I won't go to school in the bus. (North West)

A teacher talked about how she needs to provide emotional support.

> There is no way you can start in a class on a normal day without singing, playing. The children have got so much anger in the morning, baggage. (Teacher, Eastern Cape)

Additional barriers experienced in terms of health care services relate to the issue of assistive devices such as wheelchairs. One boy in the Western Cape group eloquently described how restricted his life is because he does not have an appropriate wheelchair.

> Can you see what I have shown in my picture? Here is a radio in my room and here is a TV in the other room. I listen to music on the radio in my room. I watch TV in the dining room. I would like you to tell me how do I get into the dining room? Just tell me how do you think I get there? That's the problem in my life, moving around. The problem is that my Mom carries me around. I am growing now and I am heavy for my mom. I never get

> outside, I never sit outside. Moving around in the house, that is my prob-
> lem. And also sometimes if you want to go out like to hospital and there is
> no transport. I need a wheelchair that has a control. I had one once from
> the school but it was long ago. (Western Cape)

This boy's story also raises the issue of isolation, which is discussed in the section on participation below.

Theme F: Participation, socialisation and recreation

An important theme that emerged from the discussions with the children was the issue of independence, which they proudly narrated, as well as the barriers to participation that they experience which cause isolation. Children spoke proudly about how they looked after themselves.

> In the morning I wake up and wash me and dress me. (Western Cape)
>
> I wake up and dress myself. I wash and then I go and wait for the bus for
> school. (North West)
>
> I go to school. I love to learn and know the days of the week. (Limpopo)

Comments like these were elicited through the use of a research tool that involved children drawing pictures about their daily lives. The drawings were used as a means of focusing conversations around issues in their lives. Though the children's accounts may be about issues that those of us who are not disabled take for granted it was clear that the children themselves saw these competencies as important.

Children also talked proudly about how they participated in family and community life.

> In the morning I wake up, I have a bath and I go to play. I help my father
> watering flowers. (KwaZulu-Natal)
>
> This is my home and my mother doing the washing outside and giving
> washing to me to hang up. (KwaZulu-Natal)
>
> I fetch the water until I get finished and then I sit down. (Limpopo)

They took great pride in being able to contribute at home and in the community.

> I wash the school shirt for my brother. It helps my mother. (North West)
>
> I sing in church. I lead the singing! (Limpopo)
>
> – This is cotton wool (referring to the final activity). What makes your life as
> soft as that cotton wool, soft?
>
> – It is playing netball. I play in a team! (Eastern Cape)

The last two quotes about participating in the community make an important point. Socialisation and recreation of this sort is key to the disabled child's overall development and empowerment. The children who sing and play netball have been empowered by being able to participate in community activities. Many children with disabilities are denied the right to participate in recreational activities because there are no appropriate activities in their area.

I just sit. I sometimes go to the church but there is no other thing to do for me. (North West)

Many children with disabilities live very isolated lives. This obviously makes an impact on their development and emotional health. The Western Cape boy whose story was told on the previous page is an example of this isolation. When asked to describe how he spent a day at home he said:

I am just in my house listening to music. (Western Cape)

Other children (Johanna, for example) also described this isolation.

Theme G: Discrimination and acceptance

The themes of discrimination and participation are closely linked. Children described how stigmatising attitudes lead to discrimination and become a barrier to their full participation in the community. One very strong theme that emerged from children's conversations about daily problems was teasing and ostracisation by other children in the community.

They tease me when they are playing. They say I don't know how to play. They throw the ball and they say I cheat because I have crutches. (KwaZulu-Natal)

I hate when other people copy what I do or say (she shows her hands). I get very angry when they do that. (North West)

They tease me when we go to church with my sister. They laugh and they say I can't walk but I am big. (KwaZulu-Natal)

They beat me when they meet me on the street. They beat me. I cry and I also beat them and I also get angry and I go home. (North West)

The children also described how this teasing makes them feel.

Sometimes you cry because you feel sad. (Limpopo)

The children had their own coping strategies for these situations. Many of them had learned to live with the teasing.

I tell them to stop teasing us and we go and tell a grown-up. (KwaZulu-Natal)

Others, however, found it more difficult. Withdrawal was a common response.

I just stay home and don't go to play because they tease. (North West)

Another common response described by the children was to get angry and fight back.

I am playing with crutches when I play soccer, then they say why am I playing with crutches and we start fighting. I am not afraid of them. I fight. (KwaZulu-Natal)

Children had some clear ideas about how this problem could be solved

– They laugh at us because they think we are different.

> – They think they are more clever than us.
>
> – We are not different.
>
> – Tell the government they must teach and they must tell other children we don't like what we are but God made us and we can't change it.
>
> – I can say if they are laughing at me, I can say that God made us and maybe sometimes if you are laughing at me maybe someday you will have a child like us. (KwaZulu-Natal)

The other side of this theme was the important support role that friends play for the children. All children described friends as an important support system for them. Most had able-bodied and disabled friends.

> Pearl and Tebogo make my life happy. They help me. (Limpopo)

One deaf boy from a rural area in KwaZulu-Natal described how the natural environment was an important source of happiness for him.

> I love to go into the bush. That helps me. (KwaZulu-Natal)

One common reason children who had attended mainstream schools gave for leaving these schools was discrimination.

> –Is there a school near where you are staying?
>
> – We do have school. It is only for children who are normal, who have everything in their body – those who are full in their bodies.
>
> – So who says you are not full in your body?
>
> – They say so when they tease me. I was attending school for normal children but they tease me and I am not attending anymore.

Children with disabilities also experience discrimination within their own families.

> They are angry because the other siblings were given pocket money and they were not given... The other children's school clothes were washed but theirs were not. (Teacher, Eastern Cape)

An interesting insight into the kind of discrimination children with disabilities experience is evident in the following quote. A mother in North West described how her child was not considered disabled (and therefore not eligible for a food parcel) because she took care to make sure her child was always neat and clean.

> They give food to some disabled but when my child goes they say she is not disabled because she is always neat all the time. I have to make sure she is clean every day to prevent people to dislike her, to undermine her. (Mother, North West)

This quote gives insight into how many members of the community discriminate against children with disabilities. This mother has realised that her child will only be accepted if she is clean and neat.

Theme H: Family support

When discussing support and coping strategies mothers, grannies and siblings emerged as important supports for the children.

> It is my mother who makes my life easier. She helps me by washing me. She helps me with almost everything. She sits with me. (KwaZulu-Natal)
>
> When mama and my father are not there, my siblings are able to help me with my school work. They teach me. (Eastern Cape)

Caregivers talked about the responsibility of looking after a child with a disability.

> – Hey, I don't go anywhere.
>
> – Yes, you cannot go anywhere. You have to be at home all the time.
>
> – If you go to attend a funeral you have to have girls around who will help to look after him. You have to give them rules before you go. Tell them not to allow him to go outside the yard. If he leaves you are scared other children will beat him or teach him to drink alcohol.
>
> – If you go to work you cannot just leave him at home. You find that there is no food. If he want to go to the toilet who can help him? (Limpopo)

Children were aware of this and often felt that as they grow up they become a burden to their parents.

> I am growing and it is difficult for my mother to help me. (Western Cape)

One issue parents raised was their fear for the future of their children once they are no longer there.

> I want government to build boarding schools for our children. So that when you die you know that children are safe at boarding school. The other children in the family cannot look after the disabled child. If we have boarding school it should have people who can look after them for in case I die. The children need to feel at home and have people who are professionally trained to look after them so they can feel good about themselves as children who are disabled. (Limpopo)

Summary of findings

The aim of this research was to find out how children themselves experience poverty, disability and service delivery. Through the workshops the children (and their caregivers) painted for us a picture of growing competence and a wish to participate on the one hand and significant barriers to competency on the other.

Poverty

Everyday hunger is a reality for many of the children who participated in this study. It is clear from what children and caregivers say that hunger is especially difficult for children with disabilities because they cannot always explain or understand it. In addition good nutrition is especially important for children who struggle with chronic health conditions.

Feeding schemes at school are very important for many of the children and for some the only source of food. Present poverty alleviation through food parcels is not accessible to many of the families represented in this study.

Children who participated in this study highlight how poor and cramped housing is a significant barrier to their increasing independence and competence.

Schooling

Poverty affects access to schooling for many children living with disabilities. Without money for transport and fees children are unable to attend school.

Some of the children in this study were not attending school, and fewer than half were attending schools that catered for their particular educational needs.

The children who took part in this study saw education as especially important for children with disabilities as it gave them the independence they knew they would need as they grew up. Caregivers see education as important for the future of their children. Children in rural areas were particularly affected by the lack of adequate schooling. For those children who did attend school transport to school was very important.

Finding appropriate schooling is linked to accurate diagnosis of the disability children face. This research shows that few children or caregivers had a clear idea of the specific disability they or their child experienced. Accurate diagnosis of intellectual disability seems a particular problem.

The children (and teachers) who took part in this study point to the fact that many teachers both in mainstream and special schools have had inadequate training in working with children with disabilities.

Teachers and caregivers point out that special education curricula are not always suited to the children's needs.

Abuse

A significant number of the children who participated in this study experience both sexual abuse and neglect. This abuse is experienced in the family and the community. The impact of this abuse on children's wellbeing is significant. It is clear from the stories told here that children with disabilities are more vulnerable to abuse as they cannot always understand or talk about it. The stories told here show that they are particularly vulnerable to neglect within the family.

Social security

Some children who participated in this study had access to the Child Dependency Grant. There were, however, a significant number who were not able to access any social security provision and were living in deep poverty. Also, children and adults told stories of the administrative difficulties they experience in accessing grants.

Health services

Access to clinics and hospitals was an issue for many children. Transport to and from health services was identified as an issue by children who used wheelchairs.

Specialised health care (such as physiotherapy) was accessible to only a few of the children who participated in this research. Children were particularly concerned with their need for assistive devices such as wheelchairs. Children described how the lack of an appropriate chair, for example, restricted their lives significantly.

Negative attitudes from health service providers create a barrier to accessing effective health care for children with disabilities.

Discrimination and acceptance

Children describe discrimination from other children and adults in the community as their most significant daily problem. The teasing makes them sad and it is clear that many of them have developed coping strategies (such as fighting back or withdrawal) that are not beneficial to their psychosocial growth. Discrimination is also experienced within the family.

Children asked for education programmes that will help children and adults understand disability.

Participation

Children with disabilities can participate in everyday family and community life. They take pride in being able to look after themselves and in helping within the family. They also enjoy being able to participate in community life. They can be contributing members of the community.

It is clear that many children with disabilities are isolated from their peers and from the rest of the community because of the barrier of discrimination and because there are not enough recreation opportunities for them.

Family support

Children identify family members (especially mothers) as a significant support in their lives. Many caregivers talked about how difficult it was to care for children with disabilities. There is a need to support families of children with disabilities.

Conclusion

The stories and experiences shared by children and caregivers in this study highlight the barriers that children with disabilities face. These barriers restrict their access to appropriate services. These services are essential if they are to achieve the competencies that will allow them to function in the way they want to, as contributing members of South African society. These services will also provide them with the protection they need as some of the country's most vulnerable citizens.

One of the major factors that this research has brought to light is the vulnerability of disabled children within the context of poverty. Poverty is the lead cause of secondary disabilities. In developing intervention strategies for poverty alleviation aimed at children with disabilities, it is crucial that recognition be given to the importance of integrative approaches where health services, education and poverty alleviation, for example, are integrated.

Within an integrated approach, early childhood development services are important first steps in poverty eradication aimed at children with disabilities. Often, these environments and places of service delivery are the access points to nutrition and the only daily meal for the child.

One of the main barriers highlighted in this study is the lack of access to appropriate education many children with disabilities experience. The children and caregivers who participated in this study are only too aware that education is essential to the children's empowerment and future survival, yet many of them are not going to school at all.

When looking at health services it is clear that there is a need for a continuum of health service provision for children with disabilities. This continuum has to start with early intervention and assessment (which appears to be particularly problematic). Assessment is an important first (and ongoing) need as it provides the child with the opportunity to access appropriate health, education and social security services.

The stories told in this study point to the fact that children with disabilities have varying needs. Service provision needs to meet these needs. Included within a continuum of health service delivery, for example, is the need for appropriate rehabilitation or habilitation services that could address the needs of children appropriately. In addition the developing disabled child requires increased and appropriate services at each stage of their development.

This study shows the urgent need for children with disabilities to be protected. They need to be protected from abuse within the family and community. They also need access to recourse where abuse has occurred. Also, they need protection from attitudinal discrimination within their homes and communities and among their peers. This is essential in terms of their sense of self-worth and healthy emotional development. Many of the stories told in this study show how important it is for children with disabilities to receive psychosocial support, both in relation to coming to terms with their disability and in relation to the daily discrimination they experience.

Children with disabilities need housing that is accessible if they are to be independent (which is what they wish to be). They also need transport if they are to access essential services such as health services and education.

The isolation of disability is highlighted by many of the stories here. Part of service provision for children with disabilities must be providing appropriate recreational activities and making these activities accessible to children through providing transport where necessary.

These elements are all important if appropriate guidelines and policies are to be developed for government programmes aimed at ensuring that the status and quality of life of all children, including disabled children, are improved in South Africa.

References

Barnes C. year. "The Social Construction of Disability". In Marks D. Disability: Controversial Debates and Psychosocial Perspectives. London: Routledge.

Boyden J. and Ennew J. (eds.) 1997. Children in Focus; A Manual for Participatory Research With Children. Stockholm: Rädda Barnen.

Dawes A. 2000. "What happens to children when they participate? Moral and social development". In Children's Participation in Community Settings. Oslo: ChildWatch International.

Johnson V. 1996. "Starting a Dialogue: Children's Participation". PLA Notes Issue 25, February.

Ivan-Smith E. and Johnson V. 1998. "The Way Forward". In Stepping Forward. Children and Young People's Participation in the Development Process. London: Intermediate Technology Publications.

Appendix 1: Statement of ethics

As participatory researchers with children we will:

- respect the rights of children as provided in the United Nations Convention on the Rights of the Child;
- ensure that the research is conducted in a way that benefits children's physical, psychological and social development;
- encourage children to speak, and listen to them;
- ask for informed consent of children, and their parents where appropriate, before involving them in research or in disseminating research information;
- honour children's priorities and interests;
- honour children's cultural values;
- treat children as adequate and capable social actors;
- not impose the researcher or the researcher's ideas on children;
- not use any form of abuse or exploitation for research purposes;
- not put children at risk for research purposes;
- not hide information from children;
- not discriminate against children on the basis of age, gender, socio-economic status, caste, religion, language, race, ethnicity, capacity;
- where appropriate, try to involve children in conducting the research;
- ensure research report ownership by children or where appropriate their parents or other srelated persons;
- not use material without the informed consent of the participants;
- not give out real names of persons or organisations without informed consent – confidentially of all sources will be maintained;
- not use material that will be threatening to the children, even if they have given their informed consent;
- give appropriate weight and value to children's feelings;
- disseminate findings to the group(s) that contributed to the research, in media that they can understand;
- give materials gathered from research participants back to the participants, keeping copies only with their informed consent.

Adapted from a declaration during a course for researchers in participatory research with children in India/Nepal in 1995, as recorded in Boyden and Ennew (1997).

Appendix 2: Basic information about participants

- Deafness;
- Blindness;
- Mental and neurological disabilities;
- Physical disability;
- Chronic conditions.

Note: Not all the children or caregivers could give accurate names to the disability. Hence the broad descriptors such as "physical disability".

KwaZulu-Natal						
Area and description	Basic information on participants					
This workshop was conducted in a boarding school in Port Shepstone. The school catered for children with physical disabilities and deaf children. It was a special school with trained teachers. The children in the school come from all over KwaZulu-Natal, from both rural and urban areas.	Age and gender	Disability	Attending school	Family make-up	Adults working	Social grants
	Female 10	Physical disability	Yes	Father, mother, 2 brothers, 2 sisters, aunt, brother's child, sister's child	1	1
	Female 12	Physical disability	Yes	Father, me, uncle, aunt, mother, cousin	3	none
	Male 11	Neurological disability	Yes	Me, brother, mother, brother, aunt, father	none	1
	Female 10	Deafness	Yes	Sister, me, 2 babies, little sister, aunt, father	1	1
	Male 14	Deafness	Yes	Mother, sister, sister's child, brother, father, sister	2	none
	Male 13	Deafness	Yes	Father, sister, brother, baby, me, younger brother, mother	2	2
	Female 13	Deafness	Yes	Mother, father, me, little brother, sister	2	1
	Female 13	Physical disability	Yes	Father, mother, 3 brothers, 4 sisters, me, uncle, aunt, 4 cousins	4	1
	Male 10	Physical disability	Yes	Father, brother, brother, me, 2 sisters small brother, mother	2	1
	Male 12	Deafness	Yes	Little sister, me, sister, brother, father, mother	2	1

Eastern Cape

Area and description	Basic information about participants					
The children in this group came from East London and areas around it. Three children stayed in the shack area in Duncan Village, close to an industrial area. One child came from Amalinda, a suburb in town, two children came from Mdantsane, the big township outside East London that was in the former Ciskei homeland. One girl came from Mooiplaas, a rural area about 35km from town. One boy came from Dimbaza, which was an industrial town in Ciskei. Four of the children in this group were in Khayalethu Special School. Two children had an informal arrangement to attend the local mainstream school.	Age and gender	Disability	Attending school	Family make-up	Adults working	Social grants
	Male 13	Mental or neurological disability	No	Mother, father, 2 brothers, me	none	none
	Male 12	Chronic condition	Yes	Mother, father, me, sister	1	1
	Male 13	Chronic condition	No	Mother, father, sister, brother, me	none	none
	Male 13	Blindness	Yes	Mother, father, me and 3 siblings	1	1
	Male 14	Physical disability	Informally	Mother, father, 5 boys, cousin, me	none	none
	Female 11	Blindness	Informally	Father, mother, 4 children, grandmother, me	1	3
	Female 12 or 13	Physical disability	Yes	3 older sisters, me	none	2
	Female 10	Blindness	Yes	Me, grandmother, aunt, 2 girls, father	1	1
	Female 12	Physical disability	Yes	Mother, father, sister, brother, me	none	none

Limpopo

Area and description	Basic information about participants					
The children we worked with came from Botlokwa, a village about 55km from Pietersburg. Botlokwa is a developed village and is the centre of other small villages. The main road from Pietersburg to Venda cuts through this big area. There are many schools in this area and a hospital nearby. Most of the houses are made of bricks. All the children in this group were attending a local community centre for children with disabilities. The centre was started by volunteers, some of whom had children with disabilities. The school is still run and maintained by volunteers. The new buildings have been provided by the Department of Works, transport for the children was donated by the National Development Agency. The centre relies on donations and school fees of R80 for maintenance. Most of the children in the centre receive disability grants.	Age and gender	Disability	Attending school	Family make-up	Adults working	Social grants
	Male 13	Neurological disability	Community centre	Me, mother, uncle, 2 little siblings, brother, 2 grandmothers	1	2
	Male 15	Neurological disability	same	Mother, father, uncle, 5 children	1	1
	Male 10	Mental disability	same	Mother, father, younger brother, me	1	1
	Male 17	Physical disability	same	Grandmother, younger sister, me	none	1
	Male 10	Neurological disability	same	Grandmother, aunt, sister, uncle, brother	1	1
	Male 10	Physical disability	same	Mother, aunt, my sister, uncle	1	none
	Female 16	Physical disability	same	Me, grandmother, uncle, girl, boy	1	1
	Female 16	Mental disability	same	Grandmother, 3 sisters, 3 children	2	1
	Female 14	Neurological disability	same	2 grandmothers, sister, 3 siblings, brother, grandfather	none	none
	Female 10	Physical disability	same	Father, mother, sister, 5 children	1	2

How do children with disabilities experience poverty, disability and service delivery?

North West

Area and description	Basic information about participants					
This workshop, organised by the Dicag chairperson of North West, was conducted in a village about 30km from Hammanskraal. It is a typical rural village with both mud and brick houses. People here depend on buses as their mode of transport. The village has electricity, piped water and public phones. One of the children we worked with attended the community centre where we ran the workshop. One child came from Makapanstad and the other four children came from Themba.	Age and gender	Disability	Attending school	Family make-up	Adults working	Social grants
	Male 15	Physical disability	Yes	Mother, 2 sisters, father, uncle, 3 other children, me	1	1
	Male 10	Mental disability	Yes	Sister, brother, mother, father, big brother, little child	2	1
	Female 13	Physical and mental disability	Yes	Mother, brother, sister, father, uncle, me	1	1
	Female 11	Chronic health condition	Community centre	Mother, 2 aunts, other children, me	none	none
	Female 14	Physical disability	No	Mother, father, brother, sister, me	none	none

Western Cape

Area and description	Basic information about participants					
This group was organised by Dicag, Western Cape. The children came from around Cape Town. Most attended a special school nearby. One girl attended a mainstream school. One boy came from Ceres, a rural area outside Cape Town. He was not attending school.	Age and gender	Disability	Attending school	Family make-up	Adults working	Social grants
	Male 15	Physical disability	Yes	Mother, me, 2 brothers	2	1
	Male 14	Physical disability	Yes	Mother, stepfather, sister, brother, me	1	none
	Male 18	Physical disability	Yes	Mother, stepfather, sister, brother, me	1	none
	Male 13	Physical disability	No	Me, grandfather, mother, grandmother, uncle, aunt, 2 nieces, brother	none	3
	Male 13	Physical disability	Yes	Father, mother, me, brother	3	Do not know
	Male 15	Neurological disability	Yes	Father, mother, 3 brothers, sister, me	3	1
	Female 13	Physical disability	Yes	Sister, mother, grandpa, grandma, me	1	2
	Female 13	Neurological disability	Yes	Father, mother, me, sister, baby, cousin	1	1
	Female 18	Neurological disability	No	Father, mother, 4 brothers, me	3	1

www.ingramcontent.com/pod-product-compliance
Lightning Source LLC
Chambersburg PA
CBHW080840270326
41926CB00018B/4103